ORDINARY
PSALMS

Barataria Poetry

Ava Leavell Haymon, *Series Editor*

ORDINARY
PSALMS

Julia B. Levine

Louisiana State University Press

Baton Rouge

Published by Louisiana State University Press
www.lsupress.org

LSU Press Paperback Original

Designer: Mandy McDonald Scallan
Typeface: Minion Pro

Cover image: *Earthly Delights*, by Elizabeth Pollie.
Reproduced by permission of the artist.

Library of Congress Cataloging-in-Publication Data

Names: Levine, Julia B., author.
Title: Ordinary psalms / Julia B. Levine.
Description: Baton Rouge : Louisiana State University Press, [2021] |
    Series: Barataria poetry
Identifiers: LCCN 2020033156 (print) | LCCN 2020033157 (ebook) | ISBN
    978-0-8071-7474-6 (paperback) | ISBN 978-0-8071-7517-0 (pdf) | ISBN
    978-0-8071-7518-7 (epub)
Subjects: LCGFT: Poetry.
Classification: LCC PS3562.E89765 O73 2021 (print) | LCC PS3562.E89765
    (ebook) | DDC 811/.54—dc23
LC record available at https://lccn.loc.gov/2020033156
LC ebook record available at https://lccn.loc.gov/2020033157

for Mary

Sunset in the ethereal waves:
I cannot tell if the day
is ending, or the world, or if
the secret of secrets is inside me again.

—Anna Akhmatova

CONTENTS

I

Psalm with Wren in Daylight Saving Time

Late afternoon, I chop onions by feel,
listening to crows cry to each other across the ridge.

Gone now, white recipe card on the white floor,
green sea glass found on a Humboldt beach.

But this hour I have been given back, carried out
of gorse, red flash of maples, finches in our cedar.

Meaning, today I returned for the first time
to the moment I understood I was going blind.

Months I hid from myself that the V of geese
flying over the valley extinguished too soon into fog,

a darkness fine as sugar sifted over the chard, the roses.
Now I hear the soft tick of a bird landing on the counter.

Feel her gaze turn away from mine. When she hops
table to chair to floor, I open all the windows and doors.

Sometimes we must drag our grief out of the river
and put our mouth on it. And then a loosening comes.

One morning I rose and sat outside on my lawn
under budded glory vines. There is no hurry, I say

to the stirrings of one so small it has to be a wren.
Once I let the missing in, there was possibility.

There was a heavy rain in sun—every blade of grass
blurred, and for a moment after, only shine.

Psalm with Near Blindness

i.

The world mostly gone, I make it what I want:
from the balcony, the morning a silver robe of mist.

I make a reckless blessing of it—the flaming,
flowering spurge of the world, the wind

the birds stir up as they flock and sing.
Edges yes, the green lift and fall of live oaks,

something metal wheeling past,
and yet for every detail alive and embodied—

the horses with their tails switching back and forth,
daylilies parting their lobes to heat—

I cannot stop asking, *Sparrow or wren? Oak
or elm?* Because it matters

if the gray fox curled in sleep
is a patch of dark along the fence line,

or if the bush hung with fish kites
is actually a wisteria in flower. Though

even before my retinas bled and scarred
and bled again, I wanted everything

different, better. And then this afternoon,
out walking the meadow together,

my husband bent to pick a bleeding heart.
Held it close as I needed

to see its delicate lanterns,
the shaken light.

ii.
Deer, he says, our car stopped in traffic.
And since I can't see them, I ask, *Where?*

Between the oaks, he answers,
and since I can't see the between,

                I ask, *In the dappling?*

He takes my hand and points
to the darkest stutter in the branches

                and I see a shadow

in the sight line of his hand, his arm,
his blue shirt with its clean scent of laundry,

my hand shading my eyes from glare.
There! he says, and I can see

                the dark flash of them
                leaping over a fence (or is it reeds?),

                one a buck with his bony crown,
                and one a doe, and one smaller, a fawn,

but by then it seems they've disappeared

and so I ask, *Gone?*
and he nods.

We're moving again,

                and so I let the inner become outer

                become pasture and Douglas firs
                with large herds of deer, elk, even bison,

            and just beyond view, a mountain lion

auburn red, like the one we saw years before,
hidden behind a grove of live oaks,

          listening.

Psalm with No Cure

Beneath our grapevines at dusk, I tell him
that the world is falling in on me,

a blurred unseaming of each from each
into a great sameness.

My husband reaches into the trellis,
cuts a cluster with his knife

and lays the red grapes on a plate before us.
I already know science is a religion too,

with its pantheon of evidence steadying terror.
Believe me, I'm grateful for any anchor.

Though here at the edge of autumn,
doesn't it seem that the mythic breaks down

into that battered couch we once saw in Rome
floating down the Tiber

like a boat broken free of its mooring,
except this time, one of the five white gulls

shining at rest on its pillows
will not rise into the air again.

Please don't try to make it better.
For now, there is a hunger in my lips, my hands,

as if I'd been called late to wander,
to feel by way of edges and texture

around lintels and doors, hallways
of shadow broken open by stairs.

There are too many choices
and ultimately none.

Don't tell me a station of light will remain
like a lit house at midnight

in the fields rumbled through and groaning
under the evening train.

Lost Wetlands Preserve

Close to dusk, I hear
the strange trill of sandhill cranes
setting down. Our dog whines

and tugs at his leash, and we both dream
of letting him run through the walnut groves
out to a delta roiled in feathers

and blood, stilted legs dripping
from his carefully bred mouth,
though we don't admit to it

until we have turned back to our car.
Blackbirds explode into a darker sun
leaving us now. The air is chilled.

The rancher's silo wheezes in wind.
How hard to admit time
is simply the measure between

how we eat and are eaten—
the lovely S of their necks needled
deep into plumage as the cranes

stand asleep in cold water. Brush
wolves slung low under the moon's
yellow door, staring all night from shore.

Psalm with a Four-Letter Word

A porch light burns in the flooded trailer park,
and spring is an urgency

waking in these hillsides resurrected green,
branches leafing out in shy mantillas,

even in this girl as she guns
her uncle's truck under Highway 1.

The overpass crowded with kids holding signs—
Immigration makes America great

and *Am I next?*
The girl honks in unison.

She parks beside a wall in a field of artichokes
and climbs onto the cab's roof

into a constant wind off the Pacific.
Shakes the can, before scrawling R-E-A-P

in giant block letters,
with its chilling implication, *What you sow.*

That year I commuted to work
past her tag in so much rain,

so little truth or kindness, I needed a word
to signify exactly what it should.

REAP—as in this girl means *to harvest, to gather*
beauty as it is; she means *to take it in.*

Psalm with Violent Interruptions

March crashing its green fruit
against the regiven sky, I mute the TV news

      with its body count, looped reels
    of the partly butchered and fallen.

Outside, the fields are a voice-box hallelujah—
    iris noosing cobalt blue,

      while a black swallowtail weaves
    through my clothesline hung with underwear and bras.

      Random brightness. The wrong things
    shining. Death is a plea bargain

I made under threat of never being born.
    And spring, a gorgeous parole.

      Nicasio Reservoir decanting
    a winter of good rain. A four-point buck

staring towards the Pacific, his ears like paired kites
    tugged by wind. My daughter's voice travels

      the phone lines back to me. We all believe
    what we want to believe. Somewhere,

the fog has lifted. Somewhere, new suicide vests
    hang unexploded on hooks.

The Neighbors

At least in this perfect sunlight,
Let us not ridicule her obscenities,
the cold chapel of his disgust,

nor her feet clattering down the wooden steps
scaring up the jays, his boots hammering after.

And let's not mock the multiple times they start
their cars, then stop, slam the doors,
begin again.

No, let's remember the holy was once everywhere
before it withdrew to make room for us.

I'm talking about a divinity
packing up for streetlights and inflatable rafts,

and two babies I saw once at the beach
throwing handfuls of sand in the other's face.

The way we were given everything to be lost.

How, on a good day, my neighbors
can glimpse Tomales Bay from their porch,

that conflagration of light
camped in water. Though who looks straight

at that kind of shining
without looking away?

If I ever learn to love my neighbors

it will be on a morning like this,
one of them screaming, *You've stolen it all,*
the other sobbing, *You've made a mockery of me . . .*

lest I forget this world is burning.

Lest I forget affliction
is an approximation of the spirit opening,

imperfectly seen through.

The Lives of the Saints

I stand at the kitchen sink, washing wineglasses.
In the fifth century BCE, Heraclitus wrote that the way up

is the way down. Like my five empty bottles of merlot in recycle
and the depression I'd fallen into before quitting my job—

clinical director of the county emergency shelter—
which meant talking to children after their father lit them on fire,

the foster parents forcing them to eat from a dog bowl on the floor
while the biological kids ate at the dinner table.

The saints were all about suffering: scourges, crucifixion, drownings.
Nothing but death led a saint to give up on intercession.

As for me, I'd seen my last four-point restraint of a preteen with HIV,
last feral kid armed with a blade extracted from the pencil sharpener.

Now I look out the kitchen window, remembering this one kid,
her hair a dark forest of perfectly matched firs, her angled cheekbones, black eyes.

In Catholicism, only an exercise of infallible magisterium makes a saint.
Or to paraphrase Heraclitus, the pope decides if a saint's way down is the way up.

For ten years, that girl was returned to us after every failed placement,
with a new tattoo or piercing for every john she'd tricked,

only to hang herself on her eighteenth birthday.
It was March, vernal equinox, first day of spring. *Emancipated Minor,*

they called her at Social Services, meaning no money, nowhere to go.
Did I already say she was extraordinarily beautiful?

Before her, I thought beauty was easy to see. Something the spirit feasted on,
while the saints starved themselves on behalf of the afflicted.

Now I set the wineglasses on a clean towel to dry.
Stare at the plum tree that secretly erupted into blossom overnight.

I still can't tell you the girl's name, but I'm whispering it to myself.
She taught me something true about beauty.

It is not just those impossibly perfect stars of petals detonated all at once.
It's how you see the rain-dark branches when the white lace is gone.

Psalm with Severe Neglect

I was working day shift at the county shelter,
102 degrees in the tattered shade,
and this kid, maybe five or six, had been scrubbed clean,
her hair oiled for lice. Her teeth rotted brown

from sucking juice bottles to sleep, she was busy
climbing over the dirty couch in the day room,
though when I offered, she sat next to me
and slipped her small weight against mine.

The TV was tuned to Animal Planet, the episode
where Arctic caribou shudder the tundra,
travelling hundreds of miles over snow, each hoofprint
placed exactly in the one before, the one behind,

when that kid asked, *What does love feel like?*
Soon the caribou would reach the cotton grass,
fattening their milk for the calves
that would come by the thousands,

one every eight seconds for five days.
All these years later—my own children grown
and gone, my best friend dead
after he threw himself off a building—

how darkly I remember the hole
kids like her carry in place of history,
the wild, lost self that has never been held
without being crushed. Remember how,

before I could answer her question,
that girl rose up again, frozen
in front of the TV, staring at the wolves
as they circled the herd.

During the 17 Days a Killer Whale Pushes Her Stillborn through Puget Sound

I sit in my courtyard, under sycamore and Doug firs, reading
all one hundred and fifty psalms, so that I may know

the border of God's sanctuary—redwoods
with their cool interiors, lo, even the grasslands unrolled into gold.

Above me, the air is particulate, ungodly, the red heavens raining ash.
Meanwhile, researchers further north identify the whale

as J35 from a pod of orcas starving in overfished waters.
Each time the little calf sinks, the new mother dives deep

to bring its body back up,
like these psalms that keep slipping from curse to praise,

Let the floods clap their hands; let the hills be joyful
together in the secret place of thunder.

Every dusk now, I hear the children scream with joy
as the parents let them out to play

no more than ten minutes in the bad air.
This is where I say to J35, *I am nigh upon you.*

And even if I have been complicit,
have driven the hundred miles out to sea

just to breathe in the blue air,
here in my yard I want mercy everlasting.

Here's where I set my King James on the ground
and lie down beside it. And when the mercury

passes the century mark, the heat blasting my skin,
here is where I say to the sun and flame,

Oh blighted be your great and terrible beauty
that bathes us in the world's error;

let me be covered in thy oven's work.
Let the snow of ash draw its gray sheet over me.

And here is where I call to J35, *I'm with you now.*
Let me carry on my body too, whatever residue of death I can.

Almost Blue

California at the fire-dry end of September.
My old car sped west to the coast,
as deer flashed by, and quail,

cow parsnip nodding in wind.
All day I'd been listening to Chet Baker,
amazed at how much he holds back,

how he takes pleasure in the pause
to delay the painful end.
Almost you, as if he had

all the time in the world.
As if a near miss was nothing
but regret haunting our last chance

on earth. This morning I rose,
after my husband left for work,
to a harsh light skimming the garden,

figs swollen on the tree, split and rotting
on the walk. His hands all over the tomatoes
I will taste tonight. In this crisis,

the Amazon on fire, the Arctic melting,
sometimes I have to leave my life
to know what has been given.

The dirty white of sheep grazing gold hills.
Beside them, a farmer dozing in his old truck.
If beauty was ever a defense against grief,

it no longer works—
I see the shine of this brief land
as an almost paradise, almost gone.

Psalm after Another Mass Murder

A full moon this morning over October.
And hidden by a thicket of mock orange
and bamboo, the neighbor we have never seen,

talking to his old dog. *Good girl,* he says.
Aren't you a smart one?
When we first moved here, he sent a letter

threatening to burn down our house.
Soon his weekend lunch parties will begin.
For now, a Mendelssohn concerto floats

over the fence, as if in apology
for my entire childhood, where I lost
a half hour every afternoon on a bench,

my fingers stumbling through Bach
and Haydn, believing as all kids do
that death is for other people.

Though one day I woke up adult,
without instructions for a day
like yesterday, a lone shooter killing

unfathomable numbers of people
in a synagogue, a bar, a church, a school.
I hear our neighbor sweeping his deck

as he whistles along with the concerto.
Tell me, how can desecration and music
have this world in common?

Soon enough it will be dusk,
then night with its deepening well of cold.
We will sit on the balcony,

choosing starlight. Choosing the terrible
mistakes over nothing. Listen.
Somewhere in America, a child

pokes at a piano, tormenting melody,
still convinced that, with practice,
beauty can be put back together again.

In the Morning Kitchen

In this hour there is enough glare
to blind a woman,
to stumble her into a table, cursing.

Why take the world from me now?

I'm talking beauty as you lose it—
giant kelp washed ashore in rubbery loops,

kids on a swing set
rising up like wings chained to earth,

an orange sky smoldering long past dark.

Or how last night, my husband pulled off the road—
a herd of elk in the headlights darting apart.

Four cows, five calves.

It takes a long time to give up the song
composed in divinity's throat.

Have faith, my friends say,

but mine wanders barefoot through a hard frost,
striking matches that don't catch.

My faith doesn't believe in mercy
at the end of shame, vision at the end of sight.

If someone tells her that one day
memory will be a rosary to count, to conjure
the real world when nothing else is left,

she spits and turns away

but not without waiting for me to follow
deep into the prayerful knit of the pines.

There, nine elk come unbidden
under a sweep of stars.

Psalm after Failing Another Child

I walk home through an abandoned citrus orchard.
Pick an orange, though the tree is frost burned,

the unseasonal cold like an astonished silence
after a beating the child did not deserve, but there it is—

ice lacing the pond, star frost bedded in clover.
Even the deer tuck themselves into underbrush

like blisters on a moment no one can reach.
Think of the shot-out night-lights around a soul.

Or that boy in my office this evening, staring
at the clock. Wordless. Angry. *I hate my past,*

he blurted out, *so why ask me to remember?*
Now I pause at the orchard's end, under the asterism

that composes Orion's Belt. *Alnitak, Alnilam, Mintaka.*
Each star as one more argument between demolition

and wonder. Soon I'll take off my gloves.
Bite the fruit's bitter skin to begin.

How many times must I be surprised?
It cannot be hurried. Each globe must hang

numb inside its jacket. All day, all night,
learning its particular portion of sunlight, of rain.

Preaching to the Debris Field

All summer, the bulldozer waited
to take aim at our rafters, the chimney we laid.

Winter now, and behind me is wreckage—
copper tangled in the glint of a girder,

mirror shards flashed in the hummock and slag.
Let me tell you something.

Long before the park service demolished our cabin,
there were whole days of glittering,

the raccoon and her delicate hands fishing for shiners,
the dark wick of a seal lifted up from the bay.

And let me remind you that beneath rubble
is bedrock, layer of origin.

I know you see that far shore glowering
at the stub end of a year.

But do you see too, how we sit on the sand,
watching wind brush the sea into a galaxy of light?

All I'm saying is that this world is a mortal affliction
with wounds in the beautiful.

With the sudden needles of cormorants
rushing dark out of water to stab the salt blue of sky.

Night Psalm

Beneath your arm like a fallen
    branch across my waist,
        the nothing we know. In sleep,

in a dream of a forest, a windfall
    of leaves broken and rusting,
        I walk beside the child

I am charged with
    until she quiets,
        takes my hand. Now

the moon rises as fixative
    between worlds. The city's mute,
        the call of night birds audible.

And feral, the self before words.
    Before we name, we see.
        Before the part, the whole.

Soon it will return—the beginning
    that climbs over us as light,
        unlocking your good eyes, mine

nearly blind. Behind us
    the portals, the thin places,
        the *I* before it remembers

the loss it depends on. Before
    the question can ask, love
        in this moment, the soundless

answers. The rose petals
    last night you swept into a bowl
        set beside our bed to darken.

Anthropocene Psalm

&.

Until you awake, the voice said.

Outside, the dog we called Lamb
stood in water up to his chest, barking at the pool sweep.

Sun strained through the Douglas firs. Dust rose.

I walked into the kitchen for a glass of water
and she followed.

I won't fight once it goes to the brain, she said.

*We went to the lawyers last week
and now I have the two pills.*

We wept together at the kitchen counter.

God, I thought, are you never sorry,
or always?

&.

I can no longer see

out of one eye, and the other
vandalized, cracked, and taped so that strange shards
of light fly in.

We're walking through the arboretum, the mallards
and the drab-brown ducks, young mothers

passing us with strollers
fatted with children.

The creek an odorous, radioactive green

and I'm thinking, But this is blindness,
to have babies in the sixth extinction.
The largest iceberg in history

falling into sea,
while the nearest hills burn.

And I'm remembering too, how once,
passing a crepe myrtle in full bloom, every leaf, every branch
crowned with fuchsia,

Mary stopped, gasping,
and I froze, terrified she was in sudden pain.

But it was beauty. The way it enters sometimes
like a knife and we both felt it then—

❧

In that first peach of summer, Mary's husband
brought her the visceral paradise

in brilliant flashes on her tongue,
and I thought of how he could see

perfectly, and yet, in her telling,
all through the blast furnace of July,

he brushed his hands across her skin
as if to touch and then to taste
was the only way he could know.

੭ॆ

One day pianos appeared in front of the library,
the downtown square. The homeless listened,

sprawled half-naked,
their blankets and trash bags set up around them.

I kept thinking, Mary, Mary,
as if the wrong choice had been made somewhere.

And each piano had a player
walking his fingers over the keys
of a closed black box,

so that out of darkness the spirit flickered
in the incurables too.

And blindness was just a nap
until you woke.

੭ॆ

Which I did. It was 4:00 a.m. and silent
except for the air conditioner's hum.

Lamb, still in his harness, was asleep by our bed.

Lucifer slid into the serpent. *Eve,* he said
like any salesman searching for a secret hunger,

What is good if you know nothing of evil?

The Garden was ominously quiet.
When you are a kid, Mary once said to me,
forever is real. But lately I can feel it again: forever.

And I thought of death pausing a moment
in the bodies of the living

while in the dead,
it just goes on.

Mary,
I said, to the darkness

❧

Suddenly remembering an oriole—
a bird I haven't seen
since I was a child—

that had struck itself dead against my glass door.

But what woke me
was not the nearly weightless black hood,
the brilliant, fiery breast,

but the song coming through the room,

a veering Sanctus of sound
rumbling from inside the walls, my throat,

the liminal space between
the bodies of the living
and the dead.

First Lamentation

Mary, you and I understand that a river can drown in rain,
its surface hammered opaque over the brackish roil,

until suddenly sun lashes out again.
When we talk late at night, I listen to what is left of you

talking round and round the terror—
how our neighbor died six weeks after diagnosis

from the same cancer, though of course your doctors say
there is the one in ten, the one that is you,

or is not.
Now I'm outside crying into summer's warm dark,

the courtyard fountain spilling over its rim,
water falling onto the cut slate,

water rising up again.
Mary, sometimes I imagine us as children

running like wild ponies through the blood smell of sunlight
into a river and everywhere it is yes and green

and mayflies floating perfectly between brevity and death,
until we wake, our windows thrown open then to rain.

Psalm with Lung Cancer

Because I don't know how to pray, I carry you with me
into summer, beside the creek this evening,

the wrens and whip-poor-wills amped up,
blackberry blossoms trellised white across the stream.

Mary, do you know those buckeyes candled with pollen
are toxic to honeybees?

That a coyote took down a fawn last week, and yesterday
the doe wandered onto my deck and stared inside?

These days, I worry that your every last pleasure
sharpens into a barb—a bowl of black raspberries, a hummingbird

brushed against your cheek, the delta wind set loose at sunset,
while above us, winged cells collect poison

that will sicken the whole body of the hive. *Oh God,
it's rushing in like a firestorm—I can feel the heat,*

you wept one afternoon last week. Same disease
that killed your father, though you never smoked.

We were sitting on your porch, staring at a red-tailed hawk
perched on your neighbor's spruce,

when you confessed it was all you could do
not to think of the year your father lay in a hospital bed

under the kitchen crucifix, teeth gritted,
swearing, *If he could bear it, then so can I.*

April in Community Park

Now I see it everywhere, a violence in the viridescence,
finches returning to blaze the boxwood.
And when we walk into the year's first sunlight,

the rain-soaked lawns and garden blister into shine.
We sit together on a park bench, staring out at quiet.
But I do all the talking, Mary's voice irradiated

into scars. A kidback tandem passes, one of those bikes
you can ride with small children. The mother pedals
hard upwind, while her daughter's head rests full weight

against her spine, small boots dangling over the miniature
gearset behind. Sometimes the hours of my friend's dying
are unbearable. Other times, it is the unnoticed work of love

that matters, and the wake its going leaves—a trembling
above the road as pear trees shower petals across
our shoulders, Mary's upturned face. When she whispers,

I don't understand anything, I say, *It's okay, I do,* meaning,
just now the world strikes me as coldly precise—the way
we are given to so abundantly, the way we have to break.

God Speaks to Me from the Almond Orchard

You wanted me to say it through their flowering,
didn't you? To declare my love

with these ferocious prairies of snow?
I know what you desire.

Attached as you are to equity,
you too want a chance at resurrection.

And when one of you lies face up under a canopy,
wind flicking petals from a branch,

you like to think,
This must be God's fingers touching my cheek.

I advise you to stop imagining the aftermath
as something you can apprehend.

The singular could never withstand
what the whole must endure.

Not that it matters,
but beauty was a distraction I invented once

in a moment of boredom,
musing—

before possession, what can I crush?
Not the antidote you want to believe.

But beauty in all its cruelty
piercing one world with the next.

The Anointing

All morning, the ordinary
has been filled with light. Now

a woman crosses the street, her cart
stuffed with clothes, an electrical cord

dragging behind. Her face is dirty
as a child's, her hair greasy

under her pink bandanna. She stares
hard into my eyes. Announces,

You are a god I could love.
Stars-of-Bethlehem float over the lawn

and further up the greenbelt, a teenaged couple
roller-skate, one in a dress with a white sash

where wings might have been.
Even the garbage truck reaches out

its mechanical hand with such precision,
the dogs on the sidewalk lie down in praise.

I continue on, past the poppies toppled over
with radiance. Still helpless as any god

to keep my friend on the next block
from dying slowly of cancer.

All we will ever have of divinity
is each other. And a wind

rushing down from the blue sky
cut into the exact shape

of the body
I am walking through.

Psalm with a Few Questions for Death

Why, in god's name, did you decide this
in April, when a million painted ladies

                    up from the Southern Border,
                    skitter in tiny, dusted slips

over leaf and sky—
everything that will be too soon

                    the hurried world without her?
                    Did you even know Mary

spent her last year learning stillness?
That she said it returned her

                    to the horses of her first summers
                    and the three golden retrievers

she buried under a fig tree,
troubling happiness with love?

                    So, since she found out today
                    the drugs are no longer working,

I need to ask—At the end
will you take her

                    carefully through these clouds
                    of thistle migrants,

Vanessa cardui of the silk tents,
orange apex wings, black eyespots—

                              I mean Mary
                              has been cold for months—

could you at least lift her
gently then

                              into the warm draft
                              of their going?

In the October ER

The argument the body goes on having
repeats itself in the nurses
busy with needles and electrodes,
Mary tied once more into a gown.

Just before she phoned, I was cleaning the pantry,
dumping infested flour, rice bubbling
with grain moths, black widows scuttling
through the shelved and crumbling dark.

Now, only a thin curtain separates us
from the public suffering—a man vomiting, a baby
screaming between coughs. *I wish I could believe
in God's plan instead of science,* she says.

Later, I will bring her warm toast,
hold her skeletal frame against mine, dreaming
our compost fluttering up as wing spoor, a feral cloud.
Then wait with her for whatever comes next—

blood work, CT scan, EKG—both of us watching
an elephant herd cross a river
on the room's TV, the youngest
nearly carried away,

except first one, then another giant animal hurries
to stand deep in the swift running,
until the calf floats inside the levee
of their assembled weight.

Now or later. Hers or mine. Either way,
everyone knows how the body ends.
How the soul scents the current and wades in,
singing to the heart as it drowns.

Lamentation with the Detroit River

Perhaps nothing was beautiful,
but still my sister and I knelt beside
the water flushed out of factories,
poking sticks into its green syrup,
daring each other to swim.
Something true had been stolen from that river
and we wanted the wholeness of a thing,
the world before the wound.
We wanted our bodies
to enter the current's clear run
before the auto industry arrived,
then suddenly packed up and left
those kids from across the highway
living on muskrats and crab apples.
We wanted a river that did not slip
past a row of homeless men
fishing from the bridge. That night
I pulled my father's Oldsmobile
off the road to get high,
a guttural outrage plush with drink
and sorrow, echoed off the steel pilings.
At its source, a ragged man, a fish
swinging from his pole—a huge catfish
or carp, it was too dark to know,
but I could see the glint off its spinning.
Even then I got it—his shock
that the hook had caught
this grenade of turgid flesh
like the punch line of what is real
next to what you thought could be.
Or the rip current of my heart
pulling me under every time

I imagine my mother as a little girl
before she grows up mean.
In that apartment, her father
with a match to his pipe, a cherry stink
lifting above them, I can almost see her
looking over his shoulder at the photos
in his Yiddish newspaper—
white bonfire of bones,
drift of skulls heaped together.
It's the Holocaust before it has a name,
and the mark a moment makes,
the sinker of consequence cast,
the dead weight at the end of any line.
It's who you believed you'd be
before the world dropped you
into the course of what's been done,
and named the current *your life,*
with no choice
except to ride that damned river down.

Border Towns in Texas

All week the news is about little kids in cages—hungry,
dirty, sick. Which reminds me of my favorite book

as a child, *I Never Saw Another Butterfly,* drawings
and poems by children in a concentration camp faraway.

Each time I finished reading it, I'd turn to page ten,
lay my hand inside the penciled drawing of a palm,

then set out sheets of ruled paper for writing letters
to Alena, Pavel, Len, though I never knew what to say.

Nights I couldn't sleep, I pretended I was near death.
Imagined a kind doctor to stand over me, warning,

Let her rest, until my parents shut my bedroom door,
stepped away. In summer, when swallowtails landed on

my mother's asters, I learned if I touched their wings,
they'd never fly again. Today in my garden on a bench

beside the green peppers, red tomatoes, I write
those dead kids in Terezín, the ones still alive in Texas.

Dear Children, I begin, *I know you are pressed between
two pages of darkness, but wait, soon there will be a word*

*to name the tiny weight of flies as they crawl across
your face, another for the hour they let you out to play.*

In the Promised Land

At noon, I returned sweat-drenched
and stained, entering the kibbutz
dining hall as the survivors walked out,
numbers inked blue on their forearms,

a village of names fastened inside
their black coats. Every meal
after eating their fill, they would
carry out trays piled with pita,

hummus, boiled eggs, to slip
under their beds. It marked me
during these months in the green
cathedrals of the orchard,

twisting oranges from under
branches, hauling heavy sacks
down ladders, or napping with
my door open to birdsong

and the Russians in the volunteer
shack behind mine, smoking,
telling jokes. Once, out exploring,
I found the juice factory

behind mounds of halved and
scooped-out citrus, clouds of flies
mad with fermented heat
and honey. By then I dreamt

of the Holocaust as fields of
carcassed rinds, white bandages
of pith ripped apart, juice-wet flesh
slit and pooled like blood. In a world

that gives us two souls at the start,
that winter I loved the animal one:
its lavish appetite for survival,
how each had dragged a body out

from a blizzard of bones burnt
to snow. How, in the final years,
each soul curled like a dog
at the foot of the body,

and the body dozed, blinds drawn,
oblivious to the stench wafting from
under the bed, a book open on a lap
where the world had left off reading.

My last night on the kibbutz,
I stood under a vault staggered
with stars, and the Russians,
in a rare moment, looked up with me,

red sparks travelling the white flue
of their cigarettes. When I asked
about the trays, how anyone
could stand the smell,

one man tapped the dead embers
with his forefinger. He'd heard
that, by the time they made it out alive,
all the survivors could smell was ash.

Hillside Stations of the Cross

Station where Jesus knows his mother.
Where he is nailed through his palms.

Station where I remember reading
The Children's Picture Book of Holy

in the doctor's waiting room. *Jesus,*
what if your father hides in your closet with a knife?

Station where Jesus sleeps in his death clothes,
because resurrection ends better

than the beheaded raven behind the church,
its beak stabbed into the body's folded iridescence.

Station where the faithful consider if cruelty
begins as curiosity about how the sacred

and the flesh cohabit. *Jesus,* I cried the night
my father slammed my head on the garage floor.

Tonight, I carry home the bird
and bury it under our redwood.

Station where the dead give up language,
their skeletons guarding the syntax of sleep.

Station of my daughter on her side in bed,
her ear turned up from her pillow

like an orchid with its pale spiral.
Jesus, I say to its small wound of listening.

Antidote

It was there all along
in the winter afternoons
you lay in the boathouse

under the shadows of hoisted canoes,
beside empty slips crisped in ice.
You were back-flat

in loneliness, listening
for the approximations of god
to come as deer

through white pines
at the property's edge.
Juncos and chickadees on the crust

of snow. You imagined death
as a floating into music
and happiness at the epicenter

where your mother was
no longer a broken promise,
your father setting down

his belt,
his spittled cussing.
But no, it was simpler,

it was all morning coming down
as thick fields of snow
shaken over your boot prints

until your going was hidden,
and your body trembled with cold—
then a presence

neither outside nor in, but both,
knelt down close
to ask if you were ready to survive.

Dispatch from the Forthcoming

Listen. About the train tracks, razor blades,
    stolen narcotics, your Israeli boyfriend's Uzi

under his pillow—the heft of it, how it hurt
    all night long—that's enough. Enough too,

about your father warning you not to speak
    beside the strange fireworks of that boy's

exploded head. You were just thirteen,
    age of the necessary eruptions,

newly harmful desires, and your father
    had been driving you home from dance class

when the hospital called. *Russian roulette,*
    the nurse said, when you asked.

Six boys not yet twenty. That gun
    a cannon of adrenaline, alive to gamble

with five untouched chambers
    and one bullet's worth of time. Listen.

It's okay to love the exit. And your father too,
    how he unlocked and slid the bed's rails down,

lifting that boy's eyelids, knocking a rubber hammer
    under knees, dragging a pin gently up his feet.

You stood beside the death-EEG writing itself
    in delicate needles, afraid to speak, and you knew

wanting to die is not the same as death. Thought,
    you can love the exit without leaving.

You can come into history and its sadness
        and move through the heavy room

of your childhood. You still had
        your father penning the birth certificate,

setting *Blossom* in the middle of your name.
        Remember that. When he finally drives you

home from the ER, revving obscenities
        at every red light, trying in the only way

he knows not to weep,
        use it—the word itself meaning an efflorescence,

an unfolding. Even as you sit stunned
        in the back seat of his Buick, look outside.

The rest will follow as you pass by—
        cardinals, lightning storms, sugar maples

with their leaves on fire. These October trees
        speaking in black heat and honey.

Revelation

Driving north at midnight,
under far-off radio galaxies
and I'm remembering how, as a kid
digging in the stony dirt,
my trowel unearthed a tarnished charm—
tiny replica of those early telephones
with a box and horn clipped to its side.
And it was just this Thanksgiving
that I baked scones for the homeless,
only to learn the soul was a receiver—
all these strangers talking
as if my listening really mattered,
and Joe, in his wheelchair, preaching
his theory of God that worked—
Run out into the middle of I-80,
he told me, *and I guarantee a power greater than you*
will change the direction of your life.
Salvation must be like that.
You go out thinking you have something to give
and the world turns right around
with a flooded rice field of wild swans
snow-bowed and floating.
Now rain picks at the windshield.
Wind shoves my car across the yellow line
as I drive through these long stretches
of nowhere, my radio transmitting
the crack and gravel of alien lives.
Someday, death will be an event horizon
sucking down the details of my ordinary life.
Before that, astonishment dials up
to see if anyone's home
inside the farmhouses and double-wides
I whiz past. They say that
at the heart of every active galaxy,

there is a black hole.
Before I knew the spirit
could be exhausted by beauty
as easily as grief, I was stunned—
a kid sitting cross-legged in weak sunlight,
holding the revelation
of another world to my ear.

Grandfather

The old Jew on my roof
wearing a black overcoat,
throws handfuls of matzah meal out to crows.
Mumbles the old words of the Amidah.
A violin propped against the chimney
waits for music to still his tremor.
And if this world is both barrier
and portal, no wonder that old Jew leans
against my weather vane in April—
month of resurrection, month of every dusk
I sit beside the blue fountain
with its wet lip, breathing in the liquor
of honeysuckle broken white
across the trellis. *The idea of God is buried there,*
the old Jew mutters, and suddenly
I can see it again, the ethereal light
inside that igloo he built
one Canadian winter
for me and my brother, carving and fitting
together blocks of snow. It was warm
and sapphire and hushed in there,
a wholeness without shattering.
Now the tulips in my garden open red
as the pajamas I wore as a girl
that night he put his hands
and tongue where they should not have gone.
I lost something of him forever then.
Though who's to say what is useless, what is cherished,
in the pockets of that long coat he wears
up there on the roof—the crumbs he tosses for crows,
the raisins he's saved for songbirds, praying
they might learn to trust him again
and draw near.

Hast Thou Not Poured Me Out like Milk and Curdled Me like Cheese?

—Job 10:10

Outside the garden with its fir and bloom,
I stood in the savage path of beauty, herds of elk
rutting and moaning under a cold sky.

And came adrift there, my body thrown down,
a stranger with his gun pressed to my head,
the stench of him riding a nightmare into me.

Afterwards I wore the seven skins of absence
and begged to die. Instead you let me hover
above my life for a while, then walked me

through your absolute fluency in time.
My name curled again beside me. In time,
there was even joy, a red fox napping in sun

outside my window, my youngest turning cartwheels
across the world's bright carpet. All this
I was given without choice. Myself the price

I paid for it. Death stapled into the urge of being.
Tonight, in the darkness and light of my porch,
a nightjar calls out from under the cypress.

The path out of my yard glows milk white in moon.
How hard I have fought against faith. For if I surrender,
what notice will you take of me again?

Psalm with Sylvia Plath on the Radio

I carry my transistor outside to listen.
A bloated moon breaches the sky.

Sweeping up the stoop,
I toss out a dustpan of dead flies and litter.

The human heart seems a wasteland.
The boy I cheated on, the one that bent my pinkie back

until it broke,
before shoving me onto the dirty mattress

behind my school. Perhaps the poet is right,
the moon is a bad mother. *Life is predatory,*

mine loved to say. *And you are perfect prey.*
Not yet twenty, I am a perfect fool. I know nothing

about Plath or her suicide—
have no idea that her mouth, her lips are gone,

that this is only a recording,
like a wineglass poured with darkness.

And yet this is what it sounds like
when a woman refuses to look away.

When the mind can carry the body anywhere—
can live bald and wild and blue

in this moment that stills the broom.
That smells like breath and pears and sweet decay.

Cache Creek Bridge at Flood Stage

Upstream, the creek has already crested
over berms, threshed walnut groves,
flung oaks against the bridge, torn

off limbs and crushed them to brush.
Last night, the psychic I dialed up
began by saying, *A man here—*

newly passed over—asks you to believe
there is nothing more you could have done.
Now the emergency vehicles patrolling

the levee for breaks
restart their loop. The rain too,
falls again over the evacuated farmhouses,

empty pastures, into the stream's
milk-brown seethe. I'm done
second-guessing what comes next,

whether an oracle or charlatan ferried
something of Gregory to me
over waves, if there is a god

waiting anywhere for anyone.
Done trying to see the portent
in a blue-capped medicine bottle

floating by, sandbags sinking
underwater, or which red circuitry of roads
will lead me out,

beyond this river with its vicious ardor.
Its bursting forth.
He was the best friend I ever had.

Near dark on the bridge,
I turn my flashlight on.
I don't know what else to do but witness.

Catch and Release

The oak and willow flare
until it seems fire is unsayable—
a river of late autumn light.
A half mile in, we kneel.
Gregory's hands unlatch the cage
he has carried from home.
The rat tenses at the threshold,
quivering. Around us, I watch the ponds
give back dusk singed incarnadine and blue.
Here in his last November,
before he steps off that building into sky,
I think nothing of it
when he whispers, *Go on now, it's okay,*
the wild animal leaping then into risk,
into the struggled, starless dark.

On the Yolo Bypass

I can't know where winter's gone,
     or where my old dog will go down, foaming,

legs groundless and twitching—
     only that a welter of wood ducks will rise up

from the wet earth, crying.
     Before he killed himself, Gregory confessed

that Jesus had entered his adolescence
     like a swarm of wasps, until he woke one winter,

vacated, his soul paper thin, his hammock tied
     to a tangerine tree, his mouth alive with juice

and sting. In a world that holds us hostage,
     my truck guns through the rice fields,

tundra swans bugling overhead. Singing,
     It's okay, it's okay, even if my dog cannot hear,

even as I lurch between then and now—
     the way stations, the small-animal clinics,

facedown in the blond hummock and pelt
     of him. A vet shaves my dog's hind paw

before needling in what kills. There are days
     that linger and days that burn—and if you're lucky,

a good dog to teach that suffering
     is not your fault, just a condition of passing through.

Visitation

I thought if he were ever to return
everything since would come rushing up.

I thought my blind eyes would heal,
my arms flung wildly around him,

our gladness ferrying us back
into those decades we lay in his yard,
musing if God were another word for wonder,

or if the percentage of water in a body
means the soul floats in there
like a refugee setting out for shore.

Eventually I'd ask about his suicide,

like Mary Magdalene
asking Jesus what right he had
to take his light from the world,

though today, as I walk the wetlands,
rain has made the kingdom shine.

In the distance a coyote stares,

then disappears.
I kneel to a jawbone, lift it from the fine grass,

when the slough explodes in a percussive
wingbeat of coots lifting up from water,

blackbirds slipping under sky.

§

Between worlds, it is said there is no entrance,
only entering. So he went in
and made me nothing,

though even that is no longer true—

I can see the wings muddled above me,
the troubled blessing of dusk settling down.

§

I know not to move. Not to call out his name.

I've learned from him that gone is a place,
followed by quiet.

And the coyote on the edge of the marsh
is a traveler—

his hungers unknotted,
his nature given over to a muscular clarity.

It's what I most want for Gregory now,

to be that close to whatever we meant
when we called it holy.

Psalm with Errant Joy and Devastation

I'm on the rotten deck eating a bag of cold cherries,
my lips bloodied with ripeness.

Sea light christens the grass
where the new dog lies down low in a ditch.

This morning, before we drove out
to the abandoned cottage, a neighbor hurried after me

with a poem she'd transcribed from magnetic words.
Not sure what she wanted, I can still hazard a guess,

because what is a poem, if not the intention
to pin down the river before dinner?

Already the evening's first bats
work the sky's trapeze.

The dog is a whisk dipped in mud—
wherever I touch him, I darken.

Behind me, three of our five cottage windows
are shattered, a hummingbird dead on the floor.

My daughter stands inside on splintered glass.
Lays the tiny bird in her palm

and looks close at the delicate overlay of plumage,
the iridescent rust and emerald wings,

a stippling on the throat's underside.
Only the orbitals empty.

Why not believe it was you, old friend,
that set this miraculous corpse there—

that has visited us again,
but this time to speak clearly to the devastation

the poem calls a heart,
and the heart calls a poem,

neither knowing exactly how to keep alive
anything wild and doomed.

Psalm with Higher Math

Gregory and I dive into the Feather River
as the mayflies that rise after us

vanish inside a sweep of swallows.
At the end of our twenties, we can't decide whether fidelity or desire

is closer to god—and it's not that his olive eyes
are equal parts tiger and saint, or that his torment flickers there

like a barrel fire seen from a train at night—no,
it's how he says we come a long way to know sunlight

harrows the blue river, black cliffs, and the thrush he names
as we stretch ourselves across granite to dry. He knows birdsong

echoes in these canyons, the way our lips pressed together,
once and so long ago, I remember

only the silence afterwards, pocked with regret,
the way tonight, a quarter moon punctures my pond's dark.

It's how he proves death
is a continuous function of time. And in the sky

he is falling through, harnessed to a parachute, he's alive
as the law of gravity after miscalculating slope fields and speed.

He's solving us between dimensions.
And it's not a fiery hell or a paradise, but it's okay, he says,

slipping his eye against mine to point out Vega just above Altair.
Meaning death is not the null set,

because energy is constant, though matter changes form.
Meaning, look up at the mysterium—

every blaze there approaching memory's limit,
which he calculates as the miles between the past

and his light that now comes into me
and stays awhile.

Elegy Written on a Sacramento Fire Escape

—after the Pulse nightclub shooting, June 2016

At the brim of summer, the American River jitters and trembles
far below. An emergency vehicle rockets past,

and then the ice-cream van dragging its raggedy song up the block.
Didn't we all know joy once,

and then longing like a freight train rattling after?
With the years, you will come to love this world,

a poem pasted on a light-rail car began this morning,
though by then it felt wrong, a woman with her head in her hands,

and all of us stranded in mortality,
bowed to her weeping.

Now I can hear jazz float like a bright scarf
from a nearby apartment.

Wind sweeps the tree line into glint.
Let there be a well-worn path by the river

flowing in both directions at once
where the dead stroll and talk,

or fall comfortably silent, no longer prescient
of passage,

the crowd shouting at the bartender
to set up another round,

as others, having called it a night,
walk home under the exhaust of stars.

Psalm on Vacation

Lying in the animal warmth of our bed,
I look out the window at naked ladies

in their pink tutus balancing on green stilts.
Next door, a half dozen roofers hitched to ropes

call out over the staple gun—*Sheathing. Shingle pry. Roof jack.*
How brave it seems to hold everything inside words,

when the fields have already buried centuries
under their good dirt. How brave

when the mind dresses in flesh
and memory, zipped into muscle,

strains to recall living inside the god of something larger,
but can't.

Now light falls into a softer darkening,
and rain starts up again, a tapping on exhausted timbers.

Then I think of my father, every night
emptying his pockets of coin onto the dresser

beside his stethoscope, his wristwatch.
Behind this motel room, the Columbia River wheels

its blue spool of forgotten things into sea.
I stare out at a streetlamp drowsed in wings—

a handful of moths drawn to a salt
they've mistaken for a star.

The Novitiate

I know my bare shoulders darken by day.
That deer hide in heat.

And it is the creek pooling under a willow
that reminds me the soul loves the unsayable,

while the self has named these orange petals *Starfire*.
I stand on shore yanking their stalks loose

like a rope that is breaking. Must be broken.
This is the only world I have ever loved.

But it is a child's game to believe in enough.
To remember suddenly my dream last night

of rising up, flying out across grasslands,
a trio of mustangs racing far below.

Years now, I've studied the good book,
but found nothing except the truth

of my body as it stands beside this brook,
clutching a torch of flowers, as if to signal *here*

to those three wild horses stepping through
as deer. Such slender legs, thin as foals'.

Dark lips deep in berries,
muzzles needled in-between the thorns.

Psalm with Yellow Jackets

They swarm gold behind the canoe,
as we paddle deeper
into the lake's dark chords.

All of us impossibly old.
You and your brother cast out,
reel in perch, as I press my stung hand

against a clear rock of ice
you've set on the seat
beside me. The caught fish gleam

and shudder. Once
I thought loss was the poison,
but now I see it wakes us

to what might be missed:
water striders scribbling
across the reservoir's surface,

a kingfisher high in a pine,
stretching out her wings to dry.
The venom fires up

and down my arm
until I remember enough
to know nothing

and be amazed,
as sunlight sears inside my hand,
a slight wind riffing the water.

On Pine Mountain in the Perseid Shower

Nearing midnight we drive into a cloud.
And where the road gives out in gravel,
we park and lean against the ticking car,
the dog alert beside us.
Fog everywhere.
I don't have to see it to know

that down below the sea turns and turns
as if asking, *How countless*
are these days of dying off?
Sometimes at night I think I hear a presence
whispering, *There is so little you understand,*
though it turns out to be the hushed tap
of a moth trapped inside my curtains.

All we wanted to see of the stars
streaks beyond view—
though for a moment,
you press your lips to mine,
and pull me close.
Vastness does this,
marks with fire all that leaves
as it passes through.

Psalm with September Windstorm

It gusts through the valley,
the ridgeline full leafed and trembling.

As for want and more and never enough,
the blue cables of our dead tie us into forever—

my father there playing Chopin,
your mother in the garden staking peppers.

They have met and shyly danced together,
amazed at how gracefully the soul twirls

without its bones. As for us, still clothed
with this world, we can almost forget them

this afternoon in bed, the glass doors
thrown apart to watch the swallows rise,

wings unfurled, blown back behind rafters.
And yet, just to touch the flower

nested in the between of us, death
must howl through as wind sweeps up

summer's cast-off spore. In the spell
of a season on its threshold, sometimes

a sweetness pours into a life you have
to look away from, just to believe it's yours.

Kabbalah on Tomales Bay

Because it is written
we must all be reborn

in water and spirit,
I walk down to the bay

to watch the heaving fields
of waves altered white

to blue to gold. And
walk back to our cottage,

in love with the wind
tearing apart the alders

leaf by leaf. How slowly
the crows carry us into autumn

with their feisty darkness,
and the vultures wheel out

at dusk in their black cloaks.
In love too, with the creek's

brambled trail, where I pass
three men, each strapped

to binoculars, each alone
staring up at sky. Nodding

yes, spotted nearby,
an eastern red-eyed vireo,

with its repertoire
of one thousand songs

lost or curiously carried
to this western shore.

One birder packs an
enormous zoom lens,

and one a beer,
of which he pleasantly smells.

And all are witnesses,
hunters of inventory

and patience,
which is a rare kind of hope

I decide. And climb out of the marsh
with its skunk cabbage

and bog flowers. Above me,
the white salt air

clots and veils Pine Mountain
in fog. The Kabbalah warns

nothing can be truly seen,
flawed as we are

by our separation
from the divine. And yet,

here at my door, our dog
prances out to the porch.

Then my husband,
wet from a shower,

the tribe of our days
a covenant between us.

As yet, the taste and touch
of this evening

still unbroken,
still whole.

Moths

Out of the lake at darkness,
a single lamp calls a few,

white scraps brushing glass. Slowly then

a pouring out,
and we watch them in silence.

Who can say that desire
does not throw its only body towards the unknown?

Or that before anything has come of us,

there will be one night
we sleep in a room clothed in wings

turning from every corner of sky
into a singular direction.

In the morning we wake to sunlight
and wind scarring the lake.

Every window is sugared with stigmata

written in twinned, petalled signatures,
the moths' crumbled dust.

Sea Ranch Psalm

Vast emerald all day,
at dusk the sea turns to ink.
The sky, a bonfire.
Now let it be what it must,
though you will ask, *Why?*
What did I do?
A full moon opens her white coat
to the dark matter of it—
the all-night breathing of sea,
its all-night breaking.

You were given a heart like a busted window,
and through it, arrives the gold
of late summer headlands
and one black marble
salted with constellations.
This man too, his rough hands,
and a dog the color of honey,
beside you at the end of a country.

Already the shadows throw down
their lean graves across the bluffs.
Deer rise up from hunger
and graze under the swerve of bats.

Or so the man must tell you.

Let blindness enter before you can imagine
what will take the place of your dread.

Say it will not be desolate.

Say that even in this new dark,
a sparrow begins its two-note trill
to keep count of the whole
going out, the whole coming in.

Beginning here, you will have to let trust
unfold like a softening seed.
And not just the man's hands,
but whatever you touch—
you will have to let your fingers need.

God

You know that hour in winter
when the light is salted gauze

and you stop a moment
in one of the last untouched fields
in this landlocked valley—

the new grass a rain-fattened green,
thick as uncombed hair.

Then the wild turkeys appear out of the brush
in their dark pilgrim plumage
and bowed heads

and fan out over the field, solemn
hunters of seed and grub.

This is the moment you need a prayer
from your animal self.

You need to praise
the black mud, the thickened air,
the pens of sheep in their black hoods and wool,

even the treacherous, untended road
that ends at a flooded slough.

On your old bicycle
with the jerry-rigged baskets and duct-taped seat
you pedal hard against a wind

that has come up from the southwest
carrying rain. Wind that breathes

the least branch alive,
wind that brings in the sea.

ACKNOWLEDGMENTS

Grateful acknowledgment is made to the following journals and anthologies in which some of the poems in this volume have appeared, sometimes in slightly different versions and/or under different titles:

America We Call Your Name: Poems of Resistance and Resilience: "Psalm with a Four-Letter Word"; *Antigonish Review:* "First Lamentation"; *Bellevue Literary Review:* "Psalm with Near Blindness" (winner of the 2020 Marica and Jan Vilcek Prize for Poetry); *Blackbird:* "Cache Creek at Flood Stage"; *Briar Cliff Review:* "April in Community Park"; *Cumberland River Review:* "Elegy Written on a Sacramento Fire Escape" and "Psalm with Errant Joy and Devastation"; https://www.garrisonkeillor.com/radio/pandemic-poetry-3/: "Psalm in a September Windstorm"; *Gemini Magazine:* "Lamentation with the Detroit River" (second-place winner in the 2019 poetry contest); *Hawaii Review:* "Hillside Stations of the Cross"; *Poet Lore:* "Psalm with Wren in Daylight Saving Time" and "Night Psalm"; *Postcard Poems and Prose Magazine:* "Catch and Release"; *Prairie Schooner:* "Moths"; *Qu:* "Psalm with Severe Neglect"; *Southern Review:* "Almost Blue," "Anthropocene Psalm," "Dispatch from the Forthcoming," "In the October ER," "Lost Wetlands Preserve," "On the Yolo Bypass," "Psalm after Another Mass Murder," and "Revelation"; *Tiferet:* "Preaching to the Debris Field" and "Visitation" (winner of the 2018 poetry contest); *Tule Review:* "The Anointing"; *Tupelo Quarterly:* "Hath Thou Not Poured Me Out…," "God Speaks to Me from the Almond Orchard," "Psalm with Lung Cancer," and "Psalm with Violent Interruptions"; *West Trestle Review:* "The Neighbors," "The Novitiate," and "Psalm with Sylvia Plath on the Radio"; and *Zone 3:* "Psalm after Failing Another Child."

I would also like to thank the poetry faculty at Pacific University, especially my mentors, Ellen Bass, Marvin Bell, Kwame Dawes, Vivee Francis, Frank Gaspar, Dorianne Laux, and Joe Millar, for their support and tender care of these poems. I owe a huge debt to Amy Abramson, Ellery Akers, Nancy Bodily, Susan Browne, Susan Cohen, Gerald Fleming, Rebecca Foust, Rob Hansen, Camille Norton, Ruth Santer, Eliot Schain, Murray Silverstein, and Gillian Wegener for their companionship, careful editing, suggestions, and revisions. Thank you, as always, to my family, especially Steve, whose heart is a true masterpiece. I am so grateful to Joe Millar and Ava Leavell Haymon, who are perhaps the best editors known to humanity. And to Mary for her wisdom and grace and wit . . .

NOTES

The epigraph to this book comes from *Twenty Poems: Anna Akhmatova,* translated by Jane Kenyon. St. Paul: Eighties Press & Ally Press, 1985.

"The Lives of the Saints": the actual quote from Heraclitus reads, "The way up and the way down are one and the same."

"During the 17 Days A Killer Whale . . .": the lines "Let the floods clap their hands; let the hills be joyful/together in the secret place of thunder" are from the book of Psalms 98:8 in the King James Version.

"Almost Blue": the song performed by Chet Baker was written by Elvis Costello.

"Anthropocene Psalm": the four lines "And I thought of death pausing a moment/in the bodies of the living/while in the dead/it just goes on" owe much to W. S. Merwin's language in *The Lice.*

"Border Towns in Texas": the book mentioned is titled *I Never Saw Another Butterfly: Children's Drawings and Poems from Terezin Concentration Camp 1942–1944,* edited by Hana Volavkova, originally published in 1959.

"Grandfather": the Amidah is the name of an ancient and central prayer in the Jewish liturgy. One of the blessings in this prayer praises God for resuscitating the dead.

"God Speaks to Me from the Almond Orchard": after Louise Gluck, *The Wild Iris.*

"Psalm with Sylvia Plath on the Radio": this poem was inspired by Sylvia Plath's poem "The Moon and the Yew Tree."

"Visitation": the three lines "Between worlds it is said there is no entrance,/only entering. So you went in/ and made me nothing" borrow language from *Death Tractates,* by Brenda Hillman.

"Elegy Written on a Sacramento Fire Escape": the line mentioned is from the poem "Graduation," by Dorthea Tanning, and appeared on the New York City subway cars beginning in May 2016.

CPSIA information can be obtained
at www.ICGtesting.com
Printed in the USA
LVHW110308040221
678281LV00003B/295